Fast Forwards

by Paul Ladewski

SCHOLASTIC INC.

New York   Toronto   London   Auckland   Sydney

Mexico City   New Delhi   Hong Kong   Buenos Aires

All photos are [copyright] NBA/Getty images
Cover: (Nowitzki) Brian Bahr; (Howard) Nathaniel S. Butler;
(Stoudemire) D. Clarke Evans
Interiors: Ron Turenne (5); Brian Babineau (6); Sam Forencich (7);
Andrew D. Bernstein (8); Melissa Majchrzak (9, 18); Fernando Medina (10, 12);
D. Lippitt/Einstein (11); Barry Gossage (14, 20, 30, 31); Noah Graham (15);
Sean Garnsworthy (16); Jeff Haynes (22); David Liam Kyle (23);
Kent Smith (25, 26); Ned Dishman (27)

ISBN-13: 978-0-545-00664-4
ISBN-10: 0-545-00664-3

12 11 10 9 8 7 6 5 4 3 2 1   8 9 10/0

Printed in the U.S.A.
First printing, January 2008

Contents

Introduction

The forwards in the NBA come in many shapes and sizes.

The bigger ones are called power forwards. Most of them stand between 6-foot-8 and 6-foot-11 and weigh between 230 and 270 pounds. Because they are such tall timber, they play close to the basket. Their main role is to rebound, defend, and score inside.

The shorter, lighter ones are known as small forwards. They usually stand between 6-foot-6 and 6-foot-8 and weigh 210 to 240 pounds. While small forwards can't bang inside like power forwards, they are required to have more athletic talents. Not only are they expected to rebound and defend, but they are required to shoot from the outside and handle the ball often.

Many of the best forwards in the game are so mobile and physically skilled that they can play more than one position. For example, Carlos

Boozer, Dwight Howard, Emeka Okafor, and Amare Stoudemire play mostly power forward, but they can move to center when necessary. Dirk Nowitzki has the size of a power forward, but he is very skilled away from the basket, too. And Shawn Marion does so many things well that he can change positions in the blink of an eye.

Then there are guys like Adam Morrison, whose jump shot is sweeter than cotton candy. As a result, you won't see him mix it up near the basket very often. Because forwards can do so many different things, their position is especially fun to play — and to watch.

Carlos Boozer

Those aren't "booooos!" that Carlos Boozer hears at home games. It's the fans yelling "Booooooooo-zer!" when the talented Utah Jazz forward does something special on the court.

But as Carlos has proved, it doesn't matter what people say about you as long as you believe in yourself and your abilities.

In 2002, many people believed Carlos wasn't good enough to be a first-round pick in the NBA draft. It wasn't until the middle of the second round that the Cleveland Cavaliers finally selected him. Thirty-four players were chosen before him.

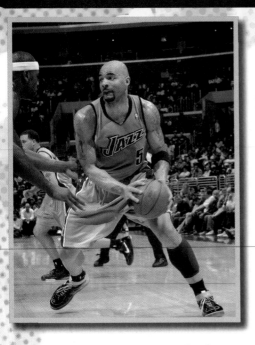

Rather than feel sorry for himself, though, Carlos turned the experience into something good.

"It's a blessing for me," says Carlos, who moved to the Jazz three seasons ago. "It definitely motivates you when you think you should have gone higher in the draft and see other players who went ahead of you and what they've done."

Few forwards did as well as Carlos in the 2006–07 season, his third with the Jazz band. He averaged 20.9 points and 11.8 rebounds per game, the best numbers of his career. And Carlos was selected to play in the NBA All-Star Game for the first time.

At 6-foot-9, 258 pounds, Carlos is a real load for opponents. He can bang with the best of them inside. At the same time, Carlos has a soft touch that enables him to score away from the basket.

"I don't want to prove anything," says Carlos, who had foot and hamstring injuries in his first two seasons in a Jazz uniform. "All I care about is how we do as a team and how I perform as an individual."

It was no surprise the Jazz were in the playoffs. Carlos has been to a lot of places, and everywhere he goes, his team usually wins a lot of games.

Born in Aschaffenburg, Germany, Carlos attended high school in Juneau, Alaska, where he was one of the greatest players in state history. In four seasons, he led the Douglas Crimson Bears to a 95–12 record and state championships in his sophomore and junior years. He was named Alaska Player of the Year three times.

Carlos played college ball at Duke and was one of the stars of its 2001 national championship team. The talented Blue Devils squad included fellow future NBA players Shane Battier, Chris Duhon, and Mike Dunleavy Jr.

Dwight Howard

Nineteen-year-olds aren't supposed to make the giant leap from high school to the pros, but Dwight Howard wasn't the average senior. In his final season, he was named the best player in the country. Dwight was so big, so mature, and so talented for his age that the Orlando Magic made him the first pick in the NBA Draft.

Sure enough, the guy known as "Thunder" became the youngest NBA player to average at least 10 rebounds and start every game in his first season.

Since then, Dwight has become one of the best rebounders and shot-blockers in the league.

At 6-foot-11, 265 pounds, Dwight has unusual size and strength. His arms and shoulders are massive. But he also can pass and handle the ball — things that big men aren't supposed to do well. As a result,

Dwight can play power forward or center, which makes him even more valuable.

"That kid is a freak of nature, man," raves Kevin Garnett, who took the same road from high school to the NBA himself. "I was nowhere near that physically talented."

What drives Dwight most of all are his Christian beliefs.

Dwight grew up in Atlanta, where he was part of a close-knit family. His mother, Sheryl, attended Morris Brown College and was the captain of its first basketball team. His father, Dwight Sr., was a Georgia State trooper and athletic director at Southwest Atlanta Christian Academy, where Dwight attended school.

Now 21 years old, Dwight works with kids near his home in Atlanta, where he attends the Fellowship of Faith Church. He also is active in the Central Florida area and even helped build a playground there.

"My message is different," says Dwight, whose hobbies include bowling, going to the movies, and

playing with his dogs, Gunner and Nemo. "I still feel that I touch a lot of different people."

Dwight had the coolest stuff of them all in the 2007 Sprite Slam Dunk, where he threw down a lob pass from Magic teammate Jameer Nelson with one hand. At the same time, with his other hand, Dwight slapped a sticker of a smiley face along with a Bible verse on the backboard. It was measured to be twelve feet six inches off the ground!

One can only wonder how much higher Dwight will go in the future.

Shawn Marion

Ever wonder what it would be like to soar above the crowd to block shots and grab rebounds? To blow past opponents for dunks and lay-ups? To swish free throws, jump shots, and even three-pointers?

How would you like to be able to do *all* of those things on the basketball court?

That's what it's like to be Shawn Marion.

Shawn is the Phoenix Suns do-it-all, known as "The Matrix," a word that means the start point from which good things happen. "I like the nickname, because it fits my game," he says.

Shawn may have a funky shot — the four-time NBA All-Star pushes the ball more than he flicks it — but heaven help the person who has to guard him. At 6-foot-7, he has the quickness and leaping ability to play either wing position, and

even center at times. Shawn also handles the ball well enough to play guard when necessary.

What position Shawn plays isn't important, really. What makes him special is an ability to do so many things on the court and do them well. More than anything, "The Matrix" is a basketball player.

In the 2005–06 season, Shawn did practically everything in the game except sell popcorn at halftime. He averaged 21.8 points, 11.8 rebounds, and 1.7 blocked shots per game, the best numbers of his career. Shawn was the only player to rank among the top 20 in points, rebounds, steals, blocked shots, field goal percentage, and minutes played in the league.

Shawn also is one of the best defensive players around. Because of his size and athleticism, he is able to shut down almost any player on the court.

The Suns like to run, run, and run some more, a style that is perfect for Shawn and his game. Because there are other stars such as Steve Nash and Amare Stoudemire around him, Shawn is overlooked sometimes. But those who follow the game closely know how important his contributions are to the team.

In 2004, Shawn was one of the players who represented the United States in the Summer Olympics in Athens, Greece. One year later, he was selected to the U.S. Men's Senior National Team. Shawn had to leave the squad because of a sore knee, but now that he's healthy again, expect to see him in the 2008 Summer Games in Beijing.

Anyone know how to say "The Matrix" in Chinese?

Adam Morrison

Charlotte Bobcats sharp-shooter Adam Morrison likes to win.

At Mead High School in Spokane, Adam, or Mo, led his team to the finals of the Washington state tournament. He scored 37 points in the championship game. In his final year in college, Adam carried Gonzaga to the Sweet 16 of the NCAA Tournament.

Yet no matter what Adam does in his basketball career, his greatest victory will always be against

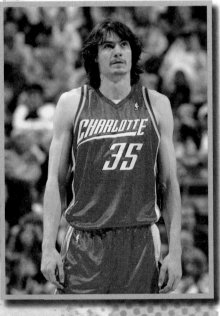

an opponent that has never made a basket, grabbed a rebound, or blocked a shot.

When Adam lost 30 pounds in the eighth grade, his parents became concerned. They were told he had Type 1 diabetes, a condition resulting in a shortage of insulin.

Adam refuses to let the disease beat him. In order to

maintain his energy, Mo eats steak and baked potatoes two hours before each game. He has to check his blood sugar level three or four times every day. He even does this on the bench with the help of a pump that is attached to his stomach.

"There are kids who are doing the same thing that I'm doing on a lower level in college and high school," Adam says. "That's an inspiration for me. You have to look at the big picture."

Despite the illness, Adam was a star basketball player in high school and set several records. Yet almost no major colleges were interested in Mo, mostly because of his physical condition. No college except Gonzaga, which knew him well. Gonzaga is located in Spokane, Washington, and in the fourth grade, Adam had been a ball boy for their Bulldogs basketball team.

In his final season, Adam was one of the best college players around. The junior averaged 28.1 points per game and was the top scorer in the country. Adam hated to lose his final tournament game so much that he was in tears even *before* the buzzer had sounded.

Shortly after the season, the Bobcats made Adam the third pick in the NBA Draft. It wasn't long before

the 6-foot-8 forward helped turn the young team into one of the most improved in the league.

To diabetic children and their families, Adam is more than the guy with the long hair and radar jump shot. He is an example of how courage and determination can beat the most difficult opponents of all.

Dirk Nowitzki

Once upon a time, the tallest players on the court were expected to stay close to the basket. You know, sort of like their sneakers were glued to the paint.

Then the NBA added the three-point shot and more athletic big men began to come over from Europe. All of a sudden, even some 7-footers started to get far-out ideas.

One of the guys who helped change the game was Dallas Mavericks star Dirk Nowitzki (pronounced No-vit-ski), whom many consider to be the best European basketball player of them all.

At 7 feet, Dirk has the height of a center. But he moves like a forward, and he shoots like a guard. In fact, Dirk is so accurate from even the three-point range that no big man has ever shot the ball as well as he has there. Every time Dirk sinks a three, he donates money to a home for abused children.

Dirk's favorite shot is the fade-away jumper. Because of his size, he can shoot it over defenders with ease. When opponents get close to him, he handles the ball well enough to take it to the hoop.

So the best thing to do is foul Dirk, right? Sorry, buddy, but he almost never misses at the free throw line.

Wait, one more thing: Dirk can shoot with either hand!

Born in Wurzburg, Germany, Dirk has as many moves as he does nicknames — German Wunderkind, The Dunking Deutschman, The Blonde Bomber, The Dirkinator, and The Uber Man. He comes from an athletic family. His mother, Helga, started for the German national basketball team. His father, Joerg, was an excellent handball player in their home country. His older sister, Silke, played hoops also.

Hard to believe, but Dirk didn't pick up a basketball until he was 13 years old. It took many years of practice for him to become the player that he is today. That is why he is also known as "Dirk the Work" to some people.

As a 20-year-old rookie, Dirk spent much of the time on the Mavericks bench. After the 1999–00 season, he returned to Europe and worked on his game. The next season, Dirk was one of the most improved players in the league. Since then, he has played in six NBA All-Star Games in a row.

Dirk took his game and his team to another level last season. He sank 60 consecutive free throws, a Mavericks record. At NBA All-Star 2007 Weekend, he was the winner of the Foot Locker Three-Point Shootout. Then he became the first European player to start an NBA All-Star Game. Even better, the Mavericks had the best record in the league.

Like his game, it seems that "Dirk the Work" has no limits.

Emeka Okafor

At 24 years of age, Emeka Okafor is one of the brightest young stars in the NBA today. But the Charlotte Bobcats forward knows even the greatest athletes cannot shine forever. At some point, they will have to do something else with the rest of their lives.

Emeka didn't graduate from college in three years with a 3.8 grade-point average because he played hooky all the time.

"Life after basketball is something that definitely will happen," says the 6-foot-10 Emeka, who reads a lot and encourages kids to do the same. "All things must come to an end. I haven't thought about what I'll do, because I plan to play for a long time. But whatever I do, I definitely will be prepared for it."

Emeka (pronounced Eh-MEK-uh) was born in Houston, and Hakeem Olajuwon was his favorite player as a kid. How could he not be? "Hakeem the Dream" played his college ball at Houston, before leading the Houston Rockets to a pair of NBA championships. Like Hakeem, Emeka's parents came from Nigeria. Like Hakeem, who stands 7 foot, Emeka is a tall glass of water. Also like Hakeem, Emeka is very athletic and has many skills.

It wasn't long before Emeka started to score and rebound and block shots like his favorite player, too.

In 2004, Emeka led Connecticut to the NCAA crown. That Huskies team was considered to be one

of the most talented in history. In addition to Emeka, five other players went on to the pros — center Hilton Armstrong, guards Ben Gordon and Marcus Williams, and forwards Josh Boone and Charlie Villanueva.

A few weeks after the championship game, the Bobcats made Emeka the first draft pick in their history. He was selected Rookie of the Year in his first season. As Emeka improved — he was among the league leaders in rebounds and blocked shots last season — his team did as well.

Quick for his size, Emeka moves so well that he can play center or power forward, inside or outside. Emeka likes to score points. His favorite move is the jump hook close to the basket — but he takes a lot of pride in his ability to shut down opponents at the other end of the court.

"If I keep blocking shots and keep scaring everybody, we'll be straight," Emeka promises.

Emeka wants to win an NBA title of his own before he hangs up his sneakers. The Bobcats main man will probably have many years to accomplish his goal. And when the time comes, he will be ready for life after basketball.

Smart guy, that Emeka.

Amare Stoudemire

When Phoenix Suns high flyer Amare Stoudemire was 11 years old, his father passed away. His mother had a troubled life at the time. Before Amare graduated from Cypress Creek High School in Orlando, Florida, he had attended six different schools.

As Amare proves, the start of a story isn't as important as the rest of it.

It wasn't until Amare (pronounced Ah-MAHR-ay) was 14 years old that he began to play basketball. Even though Amare played only two seasons in high school, he caught on quickly.

In fact, Amare was such a good player that he decided to make the jump from high school to the NBA in order to help his family. The Suns selected him at the ninth pick in the 2002 NBA Draft. Amare was the only high school player selected in the first round.

Because of his unusual strength and quickness, Amare could throw down dunks over taller players. At times, he even moved away from the basket to drain 15-footers. In the 2005 playoffs, Amare averaged 37 points per game. He reminded some people of a young Karl Malone, one of the greatest forwards to ever play the game.

Even former Los Angeles Lakers superstar Shaquille O'Neal was impressed after he saw Amare in action for the first time. "I've seen the future of the NBA, and his name is Amare Stoudemire," said Shaq, who was one of Amare's favorite players as a kid.

A few months later, though, Amare received some terrible news: His left knee was seriously injured and would need surgery. Because the 6-foot-10, 245-pound forward is such an explosive leaper, his legs are very important to him and his game. Several other players had the same problem and never recovered. If Amare played basketball again, he probably wouldn't be the same player.

Amare didn't play at the start of the 2005–06 season, but rejoined the team midseason and played a total of three games. Because he had put extra weight on the right knee to protect his bad one, it had to be repaired too. Amare worked so hard to strengthen both knees that he calls it "the hardest thing that I've ever done in basketball."

"I got so frustrated sometimes," Amare says. "You want to run, but you can't run. You want to exercise, but you can't exercise. Sometimes you can't even walk."

Now Amare can do all those things — and more. He has improved as a ball-handler. His defense is better, too. In the 2007 NBA All-Star Game, Amare scored 29 points, grabbed nine rebounds, and was second for Most Valuable Player honors.

"The struggles in my life have helped me," says Amare, who can now smile again.